THE TITANIC
Coloring Book

Peter F. Copeland

DOVER PUBLICATIONS, INC.
Mineola, New York

The RMS *Titanic* of the British White Star Line set sail on her maiden voyage from Southampton, England to New York on April 10, 1912. After five days at sea, on the night of April 14th, at 11:40 p.m., she struck an iceberg in the North Atlantic off Newfoundland. Considered unsinkable and more than a match for any natural obstacle she might encounter, the *Titanic* carried far too few lifeboats to accommodate the 2,227 people on board. In less than three hours she sank beneath the icy waters carrying over 1,500 crew members and passengers to their deaths. Only 705 survived.

No maritime disaster before or since has so captured the public's fascination. Innumerable books, movies, documentaries, even a lavish musical have immortalized the tragic events of that fateful night. The *Titanic* in its watery grave, two miles deep on the ocean floor, continues to exert a profound hold on our imaginations.

Bibliographical Note

The Titanic Coloring Book is a new work, first published by
Dover Publications, Inc., in 1997.

International Standard Book Number

ISBN-13: 978-0-486-29756-9
ISBN-10: 0-486-29756-X

Manufactured in the United States by LSC Communications
29756X20   2017
www.doverpublications.com

WHITE STAR LINE

RMS "TITANIC"

White Star Line poster advertising the RMS *Titanic*. On May 31, 1911, the British White Star Line, owned by American financier J. Pierpont Morgan's International Mercantile Marine Company, launched the Royal Mail Steamer *Titanic* at the Harland and Wolff shipyard in Belfast, Ireland. She had been built over a period of slightly more than two years at a cost of approximately £1,500,000 (or $7,500,000). At 883 feet long and with a displacement of 66,000 tons, her eight decks rising to the height of an eleven story building, she was at that time the largest ship ever built and was proclaimed by her builders and owners to be unsinkable.

Passengers at the boat train, London. Many of the *Titanic*'s passengers took the boat train from London's Waterloo Station for the two-hour trip to Southampton, the ship's point of departure. There was one boat train for first-class pas-sengers and another for second and third-class passengers. There were 329 first-class passengers on the *Titanic* and nearly 1,000 second and third-class passengers.

The *Titanic* departs from Southampton. At noon on Wednesday, April 10, 1912, the *Titanic*, towed by tugboats, slowly left her dock at Southampton. A great crowd of well-wishers lined the dock, eager to watch the great ship commence her maiden voyage. Among the spectators was a handful of disgruntled stokers who, arriving late, were replaced at the last minute by men who had waited dockside hoping to find work on the great ship.

Passengers wave good-bye from the boat deck. The *Titanic*'s first-class passenger list boasted a host of the rich and famous, the wealthiest among them being John Jacob Astor IV and his wife. Also aboard were Isadore Strauss, founder of Macy's, and his wife Ida, who courageously refused to leave her husband on the sinking ship. A number of notables escaped the *Titanic*'s fate by last minute cancellations of their passage, including J.P. Morgan himself, owner of the parent firm of the White Star Line.

Captain Edward J. Smith and his officers on the *Titanic*'s bridge. Edward J. Smith, Commodore of the White Star Line, had been a captain for 25 years and was particularly popular with the wealthy and prominent passengers who frequently sailed on his ships. He had planned to make the maiden voyage of the *Titanic* his last command, the crowning achievement of his career, before retiring. Captain Smith and all the senior officers, except for Second Officer G. H. Lightoller, went down with the ship.

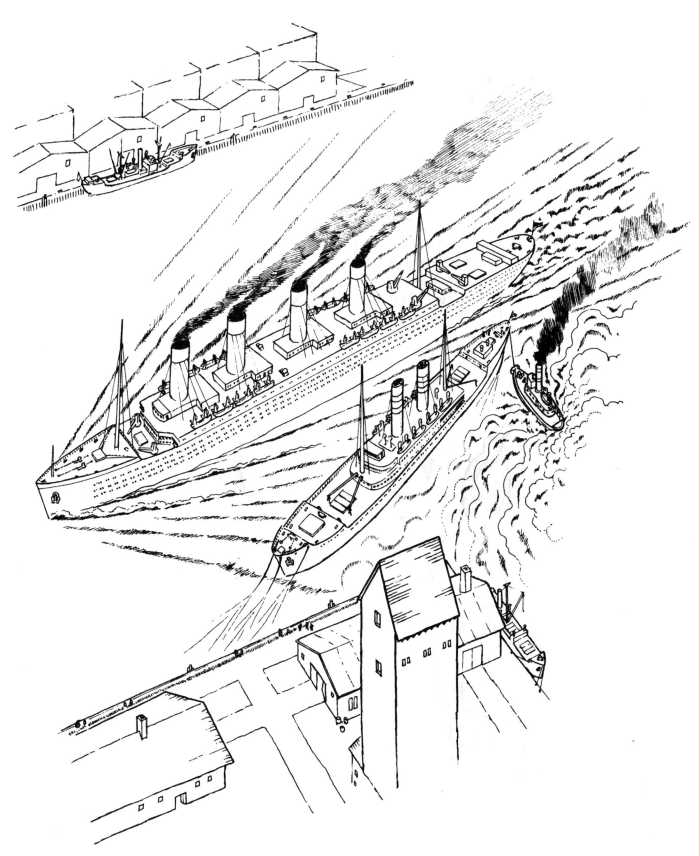

A near collision leaving Southampton. Leaving Southampton, the *Titanic* was under the guidance of veteran harbor pilot George Bowyer. As she left her berth and proceeded into the channel, she passed the liner *New York,* which was temporarily out of service and moored in tandem with the *Oceanic.* The turbulence from the great ship drew the *New York* out from her berth, snapping her mooring ropes, swinging stern first toward the *Titanic.* Only the quick actions of Captain Smith and Pilot Bowyer averted a collision. Some passengers marked this event as an ominous omen at the start of the journey.

The harbor pilot leaves the *Titanic*. The incident with the *New York* delayed *Titanic*'s departure for more than an hour and reminded Captain Smith and Pilot Bowyer of the collision seven months earlier of the White Star's liner *Olympic* with the Navy cruiser *Hawke* at a point they were now approaching. They proceeded with caution, however, and no further incident occurred. Pilot Bowyer took his final leave of Captain Smith and was dropped off near the Nab Light Vessel.

Passengers in the first-class dining salon. After a brief stop at Cherbourg, France, the *Titanic* proceeded to Queenstown, Ireland, where on April 11th she received more passengers and loaded mail bound for the United States. Passengers were lunching in the splendid first-class dining salon, a spacious expanse over 100 feet in length, boasting leaded windows and Jacobean-style alcoves.

The band plays in the Verandah and Palm Court. The white wicker furniture and trellis-covered walls gave an airy, refreshing look to the Verandah and Palm Court. Members of the ship band frequently played here. These musicians performed heroically on the night of the disaster, playing to soothe fearful passengers embarking on lifeboats. None of the band members survived.

Passengers with the purser in the first-class lounge. The first-class lounge was located mid-ship, just below the boat deck. It was richly appointed and decorated in Louis Quinze Versailles style. Here passengers met for tea, to play cards, or simply to socialize.

The Grand Staircase. Even amid the extraordinary opulence of the *Titanic*'s overall interior decor, the Grand Staircase, with its elaborate balustrades and polished oak paneling, stood out for its exceptional beauty and splendor. Light streamed in through the huge wrought iron and glass dome over the staircase.

Passengers promenading on the boat deck. Passenger accommodations included reading rooms, an elegant Parisian style cafe, Turkish baths, a heated swimming pool, a barber shop and a gymnasium. The many promenades throughout the ship, both open air and enclosed, afforded passengers of all classes the opportunity to stroll and enjoy the fair weather and calm seas.

Steerage passengers taking the sun. Accommodations for third-class (or steerage) passengers, while far from luxurious, were much superior to those found on other transatlantic liners. Of the *Titanic*'s 1,324 passengers, over 700 were third-class, and they, by far, suffered the highest percentage of lives lost in the disaster, prompting some to question whether they had been given as much opportunity to escape as the better-paying first and second-class passengers.

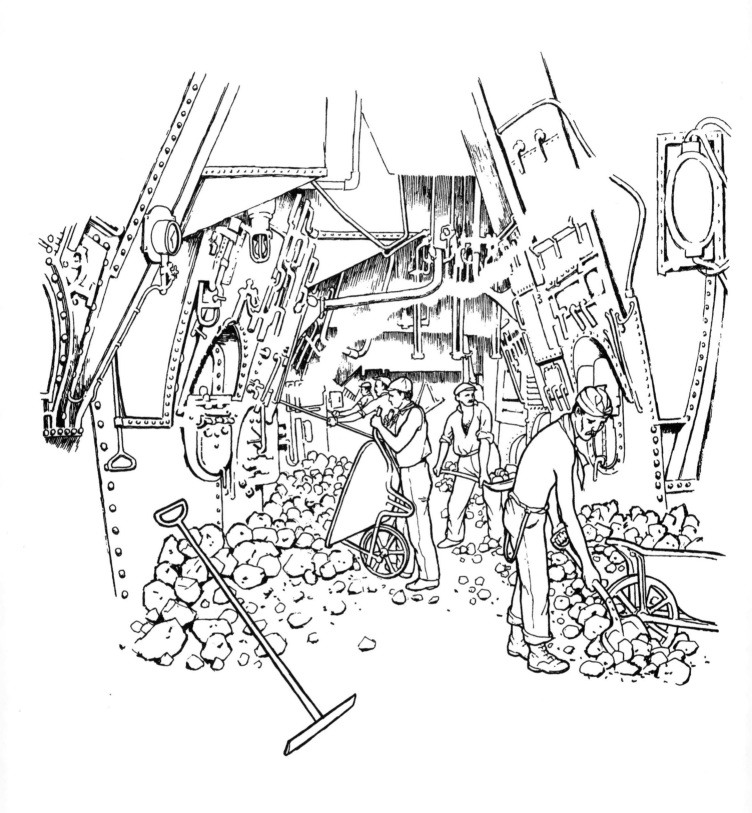

The *Titanic*'s engine crew at work. The *Titanic* was propelled by state-of-the-art, coal-powered, combination reciprocating and turbine engines. Her coal passers, trimmers, and firemen (called the "black gang") performed their grimy labor in terrific heat, feeding coal into her huge fireboxes twenty-four hours a day, one shift relieving the next.

Stewards arranging deck chairs. By the morning of April 14th, the weather had turned considerably colder and the *Titanic* was receiving warning messages from other ships in the area about encountering ice. The stewards arranged deck chairs on the promenade deck for passengers to take their ease in the sun, but for many the sun would not rise the next morning, or ever again.

The *Titanic* collides with the iceberg. There was no moon on the night of April 14th, four days and seventeen hours into the voyage, and the sea was flat and calm. The *Titanic* was cruising at a speed of over twenty-two knots. It was just past 11:30 p.m. when the crow's nest lookout reported a black object in the sea directly in their path, and rang the alarm bell. The first officer immediately ordered the engine room "full speed astern" and told the quartermaster to make a hard left turn, but it was too late. As the *Titanic* turned she scraped along the side of a giant iceberg, buckling plates, and popping rivets along her starboard bow. The sea rushed into the ship's lower hull and began flooding the coal bunkers and forward boiler room.

Sailors clearing and readying the boats for lowering. Captain Smith was notified that collision with the iceberg had ruptured the forward six watertight compartments, and that over two-hundred feet of the ship had been opened to the sea. He quickly determined that sinking was inevitable, and ordered that immediate steps be taken to abandon ship. Sailors began to clear and rig the lifeboats for lowering, as officers on the bridge started firing distress flares into the air.

Loading the lifeboats. Passengers and crew were ordered to don life jackets and warm clothing, and proceeded to the boat deck. The radio operators began to send distress calls. Women and children were the first to enter the lifeboats, though they were reluctant to be separated from their men—still believing the ship to be unsinkable. It was 12:25 a.m., just 45 minutes since the collision. The lifeboats carried by the *Titanic* had a capacity to carry only about half of the more than 2,200 people on board.

Passengers await their turn to disembark. Many believed that disembarking into the lifeboats was only a safety precaution and that in the morning they would be allowed back on board. Others immediately realized the gravity of the situation. Passenger reaction ranged from calm resignation to near panic.

The _Titanic_, sinking by the bows, sent up distress signals. The bows of the _Titanic_ sank lower and lower into the icy water, as flares burst above the stricken giant. The men of the ship's band came out on deck and began playing cheerful ragtime tunes. Lifeboat crews pulled away as far as they could to avoid being sucked down with the ship when she sank.

The *Titanic*'s radio office. The *Titanic* had two operators, known as "wireless" or "Marconi" operators, after the inventor Gugliemo Marconi, developer of the wireless telegraph. They were generally kept busy sending messages from passengers regarding their arrival in New York. In the hours after the collision, the *Titanic*'s operators sent out distress calls continuously until the end. The assistant operator, twenty-one year old Harold Bride survived the wreck.

Boiler room flooding. The collision had caused a rush of water to flood into the boiler rooms. The second engineer was in command in boiler room #6 when the water burst in.

Orders from the bridge to stop the engines were obeyed and the engine crew evacuated the flooded areas.

Passengers and crew members jumping from the stern of the Titanic. As the bow of the *Titanic* sank under the water, the stern began to rise into the air. Believing that the ship's last moments were at hand, many men who had crowded up onto the rising stern began to jump into the sea. Some were picked up by lifeboats, but others died in the freezing water.

The *Titanic* goes down. With a terrible rumbling sound the stern of the *Titanic* rose into the air as people slid down the decks into the water. Many were killed when the forward smoke stack tore loose and crashed on top of them. In the boats people watched in horror as the last survivors were flung into the icy water. The *Titanic* broke in two, the stern settling back onto a nearly even keel before sinking. It was 2:20 a.m. From the dark came the cries of those in the water. Within an hour there was silence. Over 1,500 men, women, and children were lost.

25

The *Carpathia* arrives to pick up survivors. It was just past 3:30 a.m. when the Cunard passenger liner SS *Carpathia* arrived, alerted by the *Titanic*'s distress signals, and began picking up the boatloads of survivors. One woman, still in shock, cried out, "The *Titanic* has gone down with everyone aboard!"

26

Overturned lifeboat from the _Titanic_. The White Star Line hired ships to search the wreck site and recover bodies still in the water. One such ship, the _Mackay Bennett_ found 306 bodies floating in their life jackets. Many of the bodies were buried at sea. 209, however, were taken to Halifax, Nova Scotia where they were held for identification by family members. 150 were buried at Halifax.

Second officer G.H. Lightoller, who survived. G.H. Lightoller, the only surviving senior officer, had supervised the loading and lowering of the lifeboats and narrowly escaped death when the *Titanic* went down. He later testified at the court of inquiry that followed, staunchly defending the actions of Captain Smith and the other officers of the White Star Line.

The "Unsinkable Molly Brown." Another survivor of the *Titanic* disaster was a Colorado millionairess, Margaret Tobin Brown, to be forever remembered as the "Unsinkable Molly Brown." Before leaving the stricken *Titanic* she helped women to board the lifeboats, shipping out oars and rowing, and finally took command of her own boat, helping row to the rescue ship *Carpathia*.

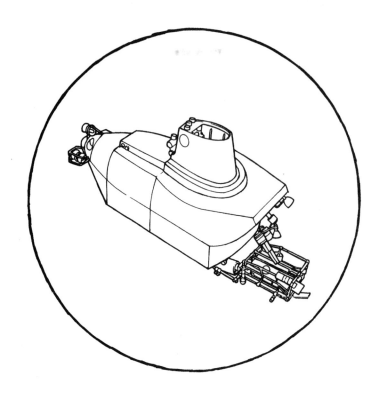

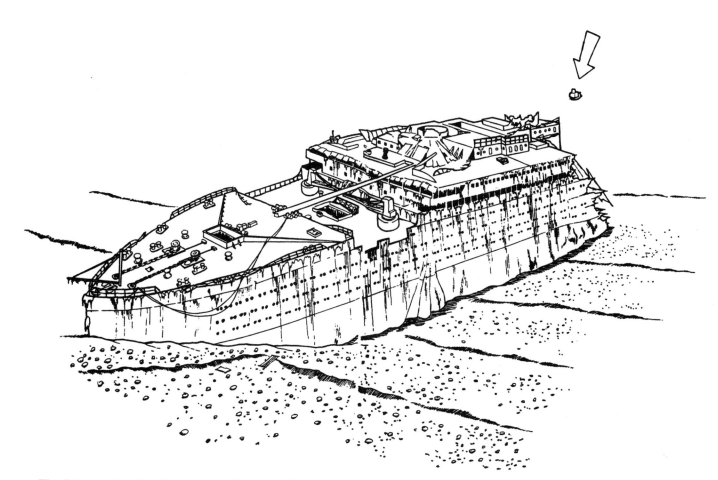

The *Titanic* today. The *Titanic* today lies two miles deep on the sea floor 350 miles off the coast of Newfoundland. She is in two pieces, bow end and stern, separated about 650 yards from each other. In 1986 scientists from the Woods Hole Oceanographic Institution succeeded in reaching the wreck site in the submersible craft *Alvin* and took a series of remarkable photographs that made worldwide headlines. These haunting images once more brought the legendary liner and her tragic story to the center of public attention.